FISH

Photo-Fact Collection

Scientific Consultant
Diane Kelly
Ph.D., Zoology

Kidsbooks®

3535 West Peterson Avenue
Chicago, IL 60659

Printed in China
101301001SZ

Visit us at www.kidsbooks.com

Clownfish

CONTENTS

Swim, Fish, Swim!

All over the Earth, in streams, lakes, bays, and oceans, fish are swimming. There are at least 30,000 species of fish—more than any other kind of vertebrate. They come in a dizzying variety of shapes and sizes: some are as long as a school bus, others could fit on your thumbnail. One thing they all have in common? They swim!

French grunt

Floating Free

Why don't fish sink when they stop swimming? Many have a swim bladder to help keep them afloat. The swim bladder is like a balloon inside the fish's body. By changing the amount of air in its swim bladder, a fish can stay perfectly balanced in the water without rising or sinking.

Northern pike

Functional Fins

Fins are important to a fish. The tail fin swings back and forth to push the fish forward. Dorsal and anal fins keep the fish from rolling over as it swims. Pectoral and pelvic fins are used for balance, steering, and braking.

Giant catfish gills

Breathing Water

Fish need oxygen just like you do! A fish "breathes" by moving water through its mouth and over frilly structures called gills. Gills pull oxygen from the water into the fish's bloodstream and dump carbon dioxide from its blood into the water.

Fish Family

Fish first appeared on Earth at least 450 million years ago. They swam like their jawless ancestors, but the first true fish had jaws—now they could bite! Scientists think that jaws evolved from bones that supported gills.

Lamprey

Jawless but not Toothless

Hagfish and lampreys are ancient relatives of true fish. They are eel-like, scaleless, and jawless. Their round mouths look like suction cups lined with sharp keratin "teeth," and they're used to suck blood and body fluids out of other fish.

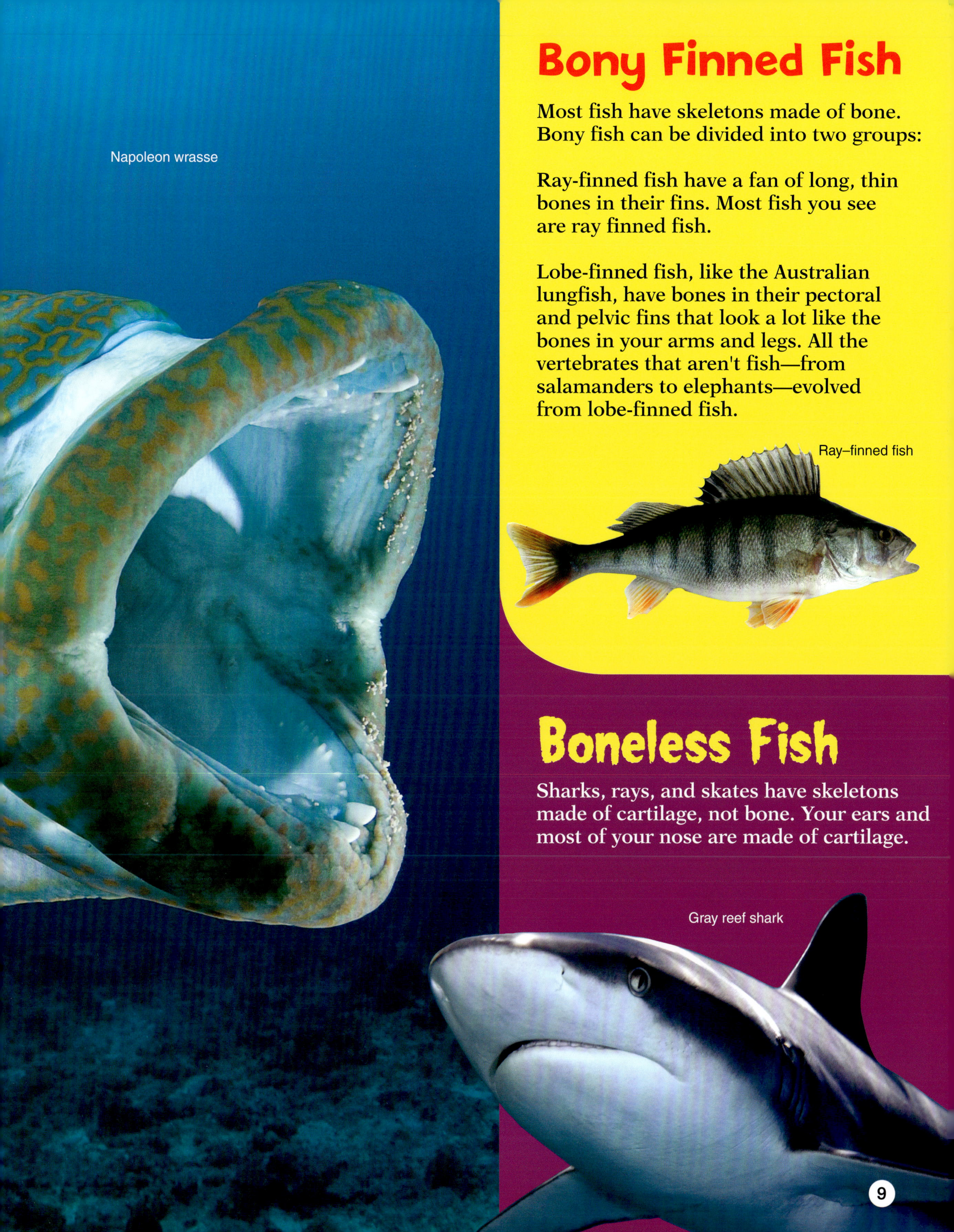

Napoleon wrasse

Bony Finned Fish

Most fish have skeletons made of bone. Bony fish can be divided into two groups:

Ray-finned fish have a fan of long, thin bones in their fins. Most fish you see are ray finned fish.

Lobe-finned fish, like the Australian lungfish, have bones in their pectoral and pelvic fins that look a lot like the bones in your arms and legs. All the vertebrates that aren't fish—from salamanders to elephants—evolved from lobe-finned fish.

Ray–finned fish

Boneless Fish

Sharks, rays, and skates have skeletons made of cartilage, not bone. Your ears and most of your nose are made of cartilage.

Gray reef shark

Sensitive Nose

The openings on a fish's snout that do the work of human nostrils are easy to see on this blueface angelfish. A fish "sniffs" by pulling water through those holes into a space above its jaw that's filled with chemical-sensing nerves.

Koi (domestic carp)

Blueface angelfish

Electric Feeling

Some fish can feel the electrical currents made by the muscles of their prey. The electrical organs in the long snout of this American paddlefish are so sensitive that they can find even tiny swimming zooplankton.

American paddlefish

Underwater Senses

Can you imagine hearing the heartbeat of your cat who is sleeping in another room? Or feeling your brother eating lunch in the kitchen? Fish see and smell and hear much like you do, but they have some senses that might seem like superpowers.

Feeling Their Way

A lateral line along the sides of a fish carries special sense organs that let it feel how water is moving around its body. These organs help fish swim around invisible objects in muddy water or keep perfect formation in a school.

Sending Signals

Fish can't talk, but they can still send a lot of different signals. Depending on the type of fish, they might make noise, flash colors, or release smelly chemicals to tell other fish something's going on. Some fish, like this oscar, can even change colors to back out of a fight.

Carp

Smelly Delivery

Fish can use scents to send messages. When a predator bites a carp, the carp's skin releases a special chemical that tells nearby fish to swim away!

Bladder Drum

Sea robins don't exactly sing, but they can make lots of noise. These fish make croaking and barking sounds using special muscles that vibrate the walls of their swim bladder.

Keeping It Clean

Fish can get parasites and infections and fungi. How do they get rid of them? By visiting "cleaner fish" like this wrasse. The wrasse's small size and side stripe tell the bigger fish that if they hold still they can get pests and dead skin nibbled away. Even fierce predators let the wrasse work around their teeth without taking a bite.

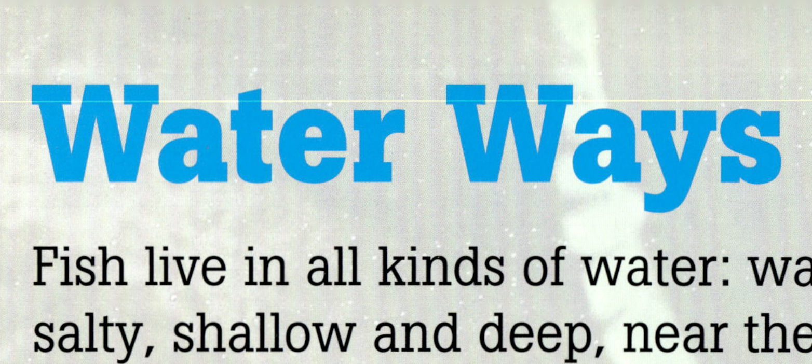

Water Ways

Fish live in all kinds of water: warm and cold, fresh and salty, shallow and deep, near the shore and in the open ocean. Different kinds of fish have adapted to each of these environments. The sturgeon family includes more than twenty species of fish, spread across habitats between the Arctic Circle and the tropics.

Sockeye salmon

There and Back Again

Fresh or saltwater? Some fish go from one to the other. A sockeye salmon is born in a freshwater lake then swims downstream to the salty sea when it is one or two years old. After living two years in the open ocean, the full-grown salmon returns to spawn in the lake where it was born.

Sturgeon

Changing Temperature

Fish are cold-blooded. Their blood temperature changes with the temperature of the surrounding water. Fish like these perch can live in a warm lake in summer and stay in that same ice-covered lake in winter.

Perch

Even on Land

The frog-faced mudskipper keeps its head above water. It seals water and air around its gills and returns to the water now and then to fill up. The mudskipper struts along with its pectoral fins and even leaps by pushing off the ground with its tail.

Mudskipper

Disguises . . .

Some fish use disguises to hide from their enemies or catch their prey. Color and shape are the most important parts of a fish's camouflage: the right combination can make a fish look like a rock, a plant, or part of a bigger fish! The leafy sea dragon has floating strands of skin that look like the seaweed it swims near.

Leafy sea dragon

Frogfish

Lethal Disguises

This frogfish doesn't have to swim to find something to eat. It sits still, looking just like a harmless sponge until a smaller fish tries to hide beside it. Then—in a flash—the frogfish opens its mouth and sucks in its prey.

Albacore tuna

Two Shades to Hide

How can a big fish sneak up on its prey in the open ocean? Its coloring can help. Predatory fish like this tuna have dark backs and white bellies. When smaller fish look at the tuna from above, it blends into the dark of the sea. If they are underneath the tuna, it blends into the ocean's bright surface.

The Eyes Have It

Some fish, like this butterflyfish, have false "eyespots" near their tails to fool predators. The eyespot tricks predators into attacking the back of the fish, giving the prey a better chance of swimming away—quick as a wink.

Copperband butterflyfish

. . . and Defenses

Most fish can be hunters and can be hunted. While they search for smaller fish to eat, something bigger is out there, hoping to have them for dinner. How can a fish defend itself? Some armor up, some hide, and some fight back! This lionfish keeps predators at bay with the poisonous spines on its back.

Lionfish

No Clowning Around

The little clownfish lives among the stinging tentacles of a sea anemone. Although clownfish are immune to the anemone's sting, the fish that want a clownfish for dinner are not! By staying among those wavy arms, the clownfish is completely safe.

Clownfish

Porcupine fish

Tough Puff

If attacked, the porcupine fish has a great defense. It's equipped with needle-sharp spines all over its body, and can swallow water or air to puff itself up into a prickly balloon. A big porcupine fish looks like a basketball spiked with nails. That sure makes it tough to swallow!

Time for School!

Smaller fish often hang together in a large group called a school. A school of fish swim together, all in the same direction and at about the same speed, making it hard for a predator to pick one fish to target.

Jack

Small Fry

Baby fish are called "fry." Most fish have babies by spawning—the female lays her eggs in the water and the male releases sperm over them. Many fish let their eggs fend for themselves after that, but some hide or guard their eggs and fry. Some kinds of fish even keep their eggs inside their bodies and "give birth!"

Surf and Birth

Each spring, grunion ride waves onto the beach to spawn in the sand. Then they leave their fertilized eggs on the beach and surf back to the sea. The eggs hatch at the next high tide and the baby grunion swim off on their own. A female grunion may surf up to six times each spring, laying about 18,000 eggs.

Grunion

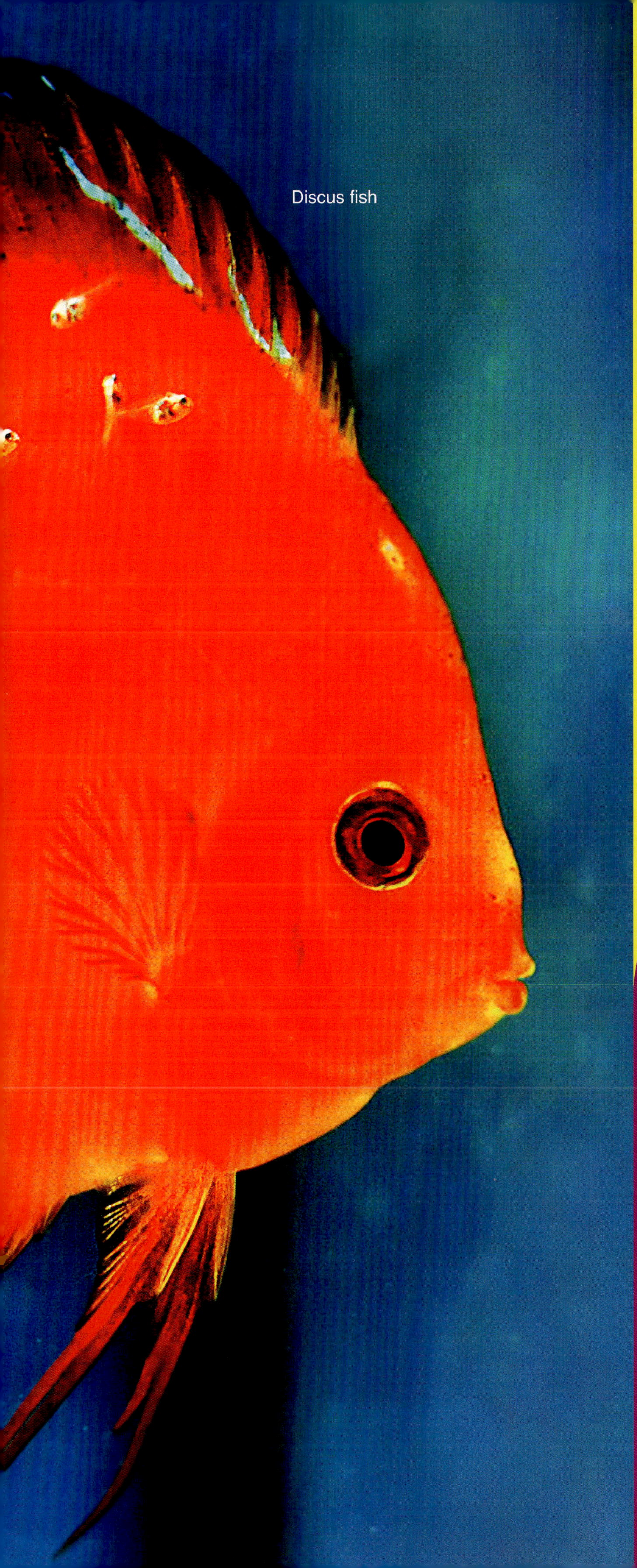

Discus fish

Siamese fighting fish

Bubble Nest

The male Siamese fighting fish builds a nest of bubbles on the water's surface. He carries each egg in his mouth and spits it into the nest, then fiercely guards his brood. The eggs hatch a day or two later, and when the fry swim away, Dad's job is done.

Guppy

Live Birth

This guppy is pregnant. Guppies and their relatives fertilize eggs inside the female, and the babies grow inside their mother until they're ready to be born.

Sharks & Rays

Sharks have prowled the seas for more than 400 million years. There are over 700 different kinds of sharks, ranging in size from the six-inch long spined pygmy shark to the mammoth whale shark. Some live in deep ocean waters, while others inhabit coral reefs or swim lazily above sandy seabeds.

Great white shark

Sea Vacuum

The nurse shark has a small mouth and a thick muscular throat that lets it suck crabs and sea urchins out of their hiding places on the ocean floor. Once its prey is in its mouth, the nurse shark crushes it with sharp backward-pointing teeth.

Nurse shark

Eagle ray

Big Mouth

Most big sharks are top predators, feasting on large fish, squid, or seals. But the biggest shark of all eats very tiny things. The whale shark is as long as a school bus, and feeds by sucking water into its huge mouth and filtering it through its gills to catch plankton, krill, and baby fish.

Whale shark

Underwater Flight

Rays look as if they've been run over by a sea-going steamroller. These shark relatives have huge pectoral fins attached to their heads, forming winglike shapes. When eagle rays wave those fins up and down, they move through the water like a huge, elegant bird.

Eels

Eels may look like snakes, but they're really fish with fins and gills. There are more than 700 different types of these long and skinny fish: some live in freshwater, some live in saltwater, and others migrate between the two.

Yellow moray eel

Electric eel

THE SHOCKING TRUTH

The electric eel of South America isn't a true eel, although it's shaped like one. It can grow to be six feet long, and most of its body is filled with special battery-like organs. A short blast of its electricity can stun a grown human being and paralyze or kill small prey.

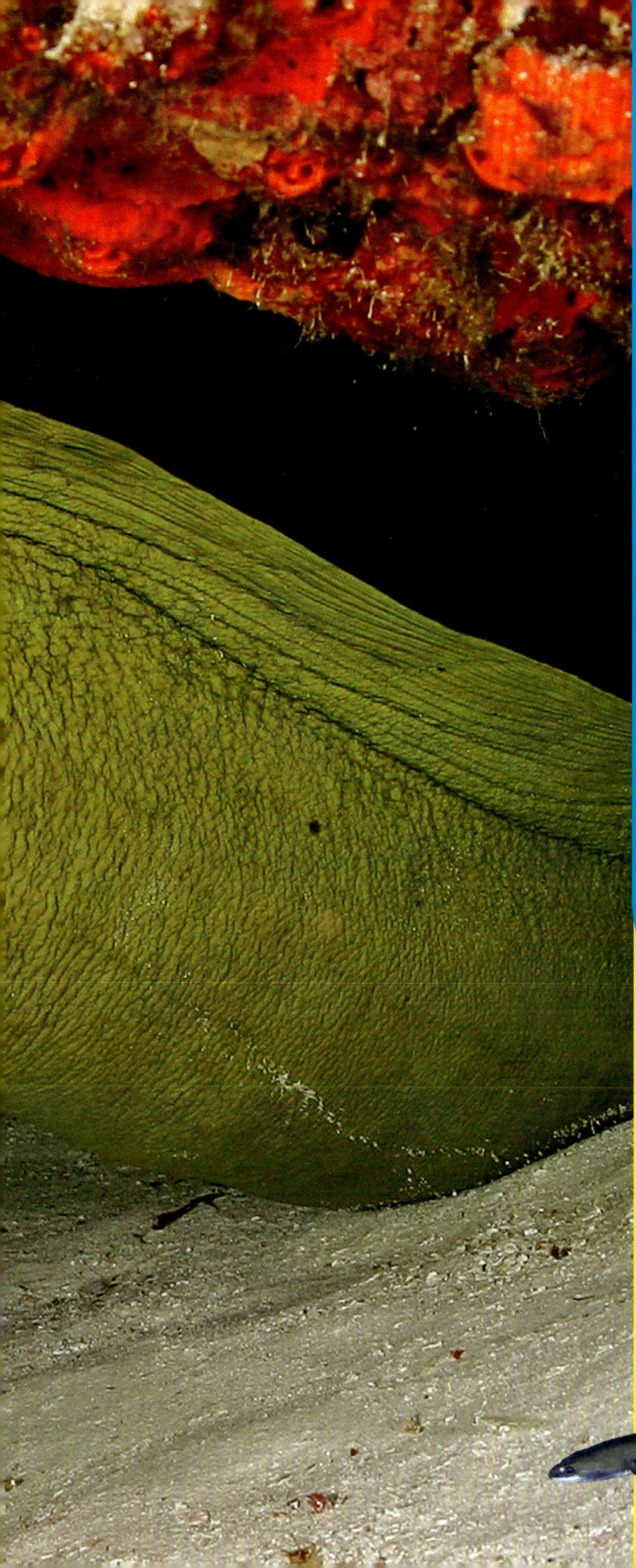

Double Jaw

A moray eel's long jaws and sharp teeth help the fish grab onto prey and hold it still. Then a second set of jaws inside the eel's throat tears the prey into bite-sized bits for the eel to swallow.

Caribbean brown moray eel

Trip of a Lifetime

Freshwater eels live in inland lakes and rivers, but they spawn in the ocean. To get there, the eels migrate—sometimes thousands of miles—to an area in the Atlantic Ocean called the Sargasso Sea.

Eel

Odd Fish

Some fish aren't "fish-shaped." They might be boxy or flat or round like a rock—a far cry from the smooth streamlined body of a trout or a carp. It just goes to show there are all kinds of fish in the sea!

Black spotted boxfish

Flat as a Flounder

Think this flat-as-a-pancake fish is lying on its belly? Think again—it's on its side. The flounder's head fools you because two eyes are staring back at you, but both of this flatfish's eyes are on the same side of its head.

Flounder

Horsing Around

The odd and beautiful seahorse doesn't look much like a fish: it has a head like a delicate horse, a grasping tail like a monkey, and a pouch like a kangaroo. But it is a true fish that uses its long narrow snout to suck up tiny shrimp.

Seahorse

Remora

Free Ride

A remora doesn't look too strange until you notice the powerful suction disc on top of its head. The disc lets the remora stick to animals like sharks or turtles. The fish gets a free ride, plus any food that the larger animal drops. Now that's using its head!

Fish & People

People may keep fish as pets or visit aquariums to watch them swim, and some people see fish on their dinner plates. Food fish are caught in freshwater and saltwater, both by people catching a few for fun and by people working on large commercial fishing boats.

Fish Farms

About one-third of the fish people eat are raised on farms. People farm freshwater fish like trout or catfish as well as marine fish like salmon or seabass, raising them in large ponds or inside pens immersed in larger bodies of water.

Changing the Food Chain

People don't have to hunt fish to reduce their numbers. A recent study found that there are fewer sharks on the reefs near where people live. Because people are catching the same fish the sharks would eat, the sharks go hungry.

Reef shark

Artificial Habitats

Some people try to give fish new places to live by deliberately sinking old train cars, ships, and even oil rigs to form artificial reefs. Over time, these man-made structures are covered by algae and corals and give fish a place to hide from their predators.

GLOSSARY

Anal fin: Fin on the rear underside of a fish; along with the dorsal fin, it keeps a fish stable in the water.

Camouflage: The way an animal disguises and protects itself by blending with its surroundings.

Cartilage: Firm, flexible gristle that can make up part (or all) of a skeleton. Human ears and noses contain cartilage.

Cold-blooded: Having a body temperature that is not regulated internally but adapts to the temperature of surrounding air or water.

Dorsal fin: Large fin on the upper back of a fish that keeps the fish from rolling over.

Eyespot: False eye, larger than a real eye, located near the tail of a fish; used to fool predators into thinking that the fish is too big to eat.

Fin: A stiff appendage on a fish that helps it move forward, balance, steer, brake, and stay on course while swimming.

Fry: Baby fish.

Gills: The breathing organs of fish and other water animals.

Habitat: The natural home of an animal or plant.

Keratin: A hard material that makes up nails, horns, and hagfish and lamprey "teeth."

Lateral line: Sense organs on the sides of fish that are used to detect movements of the water around it.

Parasite: An organism that depends on another animal for food or support.

Paralyze: To make incapable of movement.

Pectoral fins: Fins on both sides of a fish's chest that are used for balance or propulsion.

Pelvic fins: A pair of fins on a fish's underside that help it balance, steer, and stop.

Plankton: Tiny animals and plants living in the sea that are the basic food for larger sea animals, such as whales.

Predator: An animal that hunts other animals for food.

Prey: An animal that is hunted by other animals.

School: A large number of fish swimming together.

Spawn: To produce fertilized eggs. A female fish places her eggs in the water, then the male fertilizes them.

Swim bladder: An organ in most bony fish that contains oxygen and helps the fish stay in one place without floating upward or sinking.

Vertebrate: Animals that have a backbone.

Vibrations: Quivering or trembling motions that can be heard or felt.

Zooplankton: Microscopic animals that float freely in bodies of water.